A SPACESHIP

Like a spaceship, the Earth has only a limited amount of fuel and supplies. When they have run out, they cannot be replaced.

THEN WHAT WILL WE DO?

Find out what **YOU** can do about

* **Saving raw materials!**
* **Protecting the environment!**
* **Waste disposal!**
* **Saving energy!**

WHAT HAVE YOU THROWN AWAY TODAY?

WHAT IS RUBBISH?

Most of the things you throw away as rubbish were useful when they were bought.

When you buy cornflakes you have to buy the packet as well as the cereals inside!

 And then there's that horrible shirt. Somebody else might love it!

The main thing wrong with rubbish is...

MOST PEOPLE THINK IT'S RUBBISH!

BUT... clever people know that rubbish is

VALUABLE!

USEFUL!

WORTH SAVING!

So let's dig through some of this stuff we call rubbish and see who's right!..

What would it be like to live in a dustbin?
It would be DARK and...

SMELLY!

Smelly gases are given off when the things we throw away start to rot.

THE SMELL BIN

What is your least favourite smell?

Smelly socks?

Mum's perfume?

Rotting vegetables?

POO!

The bottom
of your
school bag?

Rotten eggs?

Dad's aftershave?

Horse manure?

What else can you think of?

WHAT A LOAD OF RUBBISH!

TRASH FACT

During a year, an average family will probably throw away 1.5 tonnes of rubbish. That's like throwing away HALF AN ELEPHANT every year!

TRASH FACT

Among the things thrown away each year in the United States of America are...
50 billion metal cans,
26 billion bottles,
65 billion bottle tops!
7 million motor cars are scrapped!

TRASH FACT

If you heaped up all the rubbish thrown away in Britain each year, it would cover 60 soccer pitches with piles of waste 500 metres high.

SCRATCH FACT

Did you know that every time you scratch an itch, you let loose a very small cloud of dead skin and hair? This is what makes a lot of the dust in a house!

DO WE NEED TO THROW AWAY SO MANY THINGS?

Most of the rubbish in your dustbin is empty containers and packaging. For example, every plastic bottle you throw away costs money to make. When you buy the drink you have to pay for the bottle as well.When you throw the bottle away it's like putting money down a drain. If it were your pocket money, you'd have to be crazy to do that!

We spend millions of pounds on getting rid of rubbish. Dustbin lorries like this cost a fortune to build and use.

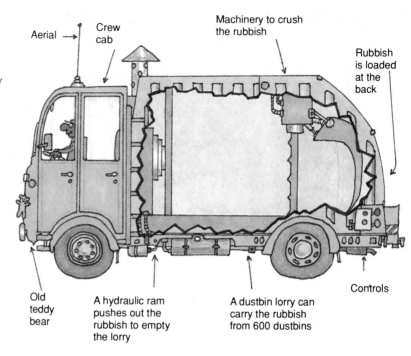

Aerial → Crew cab

Machinery to crush the rubbish

Rubbish is loaded at the back

Old teddy bear

A hydraulic ram pushes out the rubbish to empty the lorry

A dustbin lorry can carry the rubbish from 600 dustbins

Controls

After the rubbish is collected it's often buried in huge holes in the ground. These holes are usually called rubbish tips. People who dig these holes for dumping rubbish call them landfill sites. They think this sounds better than 'rubbish tips'.

BUT...

here are three reasons why landfill is a bad idea...

REASON 1   We are running out of places to dump rubbish!..

The landfill site's full up... so we're delivering rubbish today!

REASON 2   Remember the smell of rotting rubbish?
One of the gases has no smell!..

METHANE GAS

Methane gas is
dangerous because
it's poisonous and

EXPLOSIVE!

REASON 3   Animals which set up home on landfill sites can spread
diseases. A rubbish tip is a great place to live for mice, insects
and rats! In fact it's like one big holiday camp for them!..

Rubbish is often burnt to save space. If you look at a bonfire before it has been lit, it looks like this.

When it has been burnt it makes a smaller pile, like this.

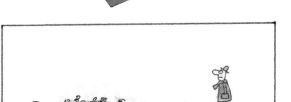

Some towns burn their household rubbish in a special factory. These buildings have a large oven inside called a combuster. Using these combusters helps to solve the rat problem!

Power stations use coal, oil, gas or nuclear fuel to give us electricity and hot water. A combuster can do the same job much more cheaply by burning rubbish instead!

PLUS...

The left-over ashes can be used to make fertilizers to help plants grow better.

Sometimes rubbish is only half burnt by mistake.
When this happens, the combuster can pour out smoke and deadly gases!..

RUBBISH DUMP

Landfill's no good!

No..it's bad for the land, and it's a waste of good rubbish!

Combusters are better!

But they can be bad for the air.

What about seafill?

What's that?

It's like landfill, except that rubbish is dumped in the sea instead of in the land!

Many towns and cities dump their rubbish in the sea. Careless dumping of waste makes the ocean more polluted!

Mum! will I get fingers when I grow up?

FISH FINGERS

The windscreen wipers don't work!

Look it's uncle Terry!

Poor old Terry!

It's raining cat and dog food cans!

We must be more careful about what is thrown away. Waste chemicals and other rubbish dumped in the sea can easily poison fish for years afterwards. And then...

WHO EATS THE FISH?

One way to use rubbish is called composting. Rubbish is stored in huge containers where it rots away. Then it's mixed with chemicals to make fertilizers. This works well for most rubbish. But many types of plastics don't rot away, and metals have to be taken out so that they don't poison the fertilizer. This all takes a long time and a lot of good rubbish is still wasted.

It's better to use things over and over again...

> We love compost!

An average milk bottle is used 25 times before it breaks or gets lost!

1 bottle = 25 milk cartons thrown away

Gardeners use potato peelings and other vegetable matter to make compost which they add to the soil.

HOW TO MAKE A COMPOST HEAP IN A DUSTBIN...

1. Making compost is a messy job.
Get an old dustbin and put it in an unused part of your garden.
Ask an adult to make two rows of drainage holes in it.

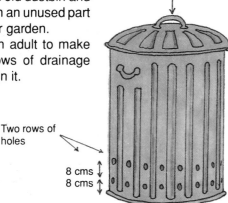

Old metal or plastic dustbin

Two rows of holes

8 cms
8 cms

2. Then you need...
Sand and small bits of broken pottery.
Some pieces of wood.
Some brandling worms. Get these from a fishing shop.
Some peat from a garden centre.

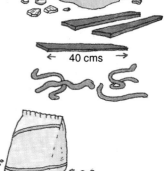

← 40 cms →

3. Put them in the bin like this...

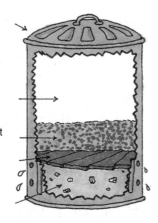

Add water at the top from time to time

Space for waste vegetable matter

Some peat

Strips of wood

Sand and broken pottery

4. Add your chopped up waste vegetables. Small amounts of bread and dairy products are good for the worms. Put the worms in the waste food. They eat the vegetable matter and turn it into soil which has a lot of nitrogen in it. Plants need nitrogen to grow properly.

POINTS TO NOTE:

Sort out the worms and put them back in the bin when you use the compost.

You can keep the same sand and wood for each batch of compost.

It will take a few months to make useful compost, but the worms live a long time, so you can keep on using the compost bin for ages!

Using things over and over again is called

RECYCLING!

Almost everything you put in your dustbin can be recycled.
BUT...only a small amount of this rubbish is recycled. In Britain for example, we could save about about 750 million pounds every year by recycling the items which we just throw away.
That's a stack of £10 notes 10 kilometres high!

ALSO: about the same amount is spent on waste disposal!

CHARITY SPOT

Some charities make a lot of money from recycling. They will be pleased to take your old spectacles, aluminium foil, old stamps, foreign coins and so on. Why not take that unwanted shirt to a charity shop instead of throwing it away? The charity shop can sell it and use the money to help people.

Glasses — Ring-pulls — Bottle tops — Old stamps — Foreign coins — Hats — Gloves — Scarves

There are lots of charities.
Look for them in the phone book.
Choose your favourite charity and support it with...

RECYCLING!

GO FOR GOLD!

In the old days, prospectors travelled for miles to look for gold.
You only have to travel to your dustbin to find your gold mine!
Here's what you need to be

THE WELL-DRESSED RECYCLER

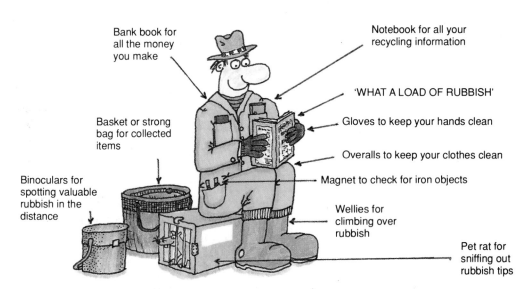

Bank book for all the money you make

Notebook for all your recycling information

'WHAT A LOAD OF RUBBISH'

Gloves to keep your hands clean

Basket or strong bag for collected items

Overalls to keep your clothes clean

Magnet to check for iron objects

Binoculars for spotting valuable rubbish in the distance

Wellies for climbing over rubbish

Pet rat for sniffing out rubbish tips

HOW TO MAKE A RECYCLING NOTEBOOK

1. Get about 20 pieces of scrap paper. Unused pages in old exercise books are best. The insides of used envelopes will do.

2. Find a piece of stiff cardboard about twice as wide as the paper.

3. Get an old shoelace.

4. Put them all together like this...

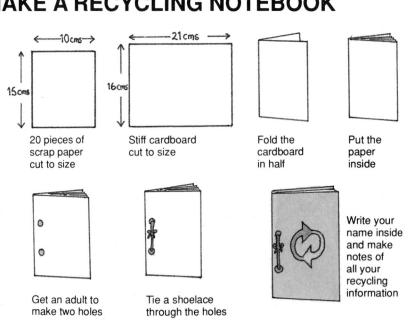

20 pieces of scrap paper cut to size

Stiff cardboard cut to size

Fold the cardboard in half

Put the paper inside

Get an adult to make two holes

Tie a shoelace through the holes

Write your name inside and make notes of all your recycling information

Is there a **BOTTLE BANK** near your house?

A bottle bank isn't a place for bottles to take their money!

Bottle banks look like this...

You use them like post boxes, except that you put bottles and jars into the holes instead of letters.

It's very important to put your bottles in the correct bottle bank. Don't mix up the colours!

Even famous people use bottle banks. Prince Charles has set up a bottle bank at...

BUCKINGHAM PALACE!..

WHAT YOU CAN DO...

You could write to your town council and ask them to set up a bottle bank in your neighbourhood.

THE LIFE-CYCLE OF A BOTTLE

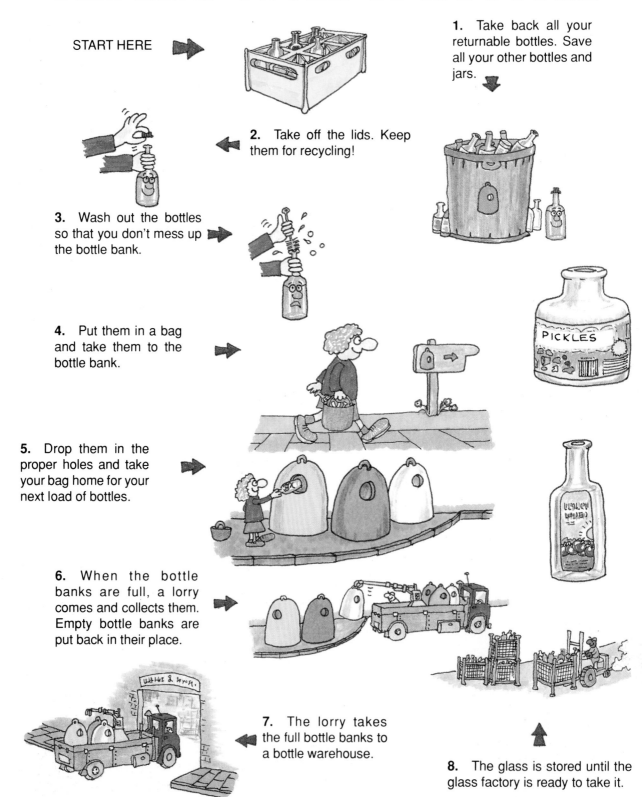

START HERE

1. Take back all your returnable bottles. Save all your other bottles and jars.

2. Take off the lids. Keep them for recycling!

3. Wash out the bottles so that you don't mess up the bottle bank.

4. Put them in a bag and take them to the bottle bank.

5. Drop them in the proper holes and take your bag home for your next load of bottles.

6. When the bottle banks are full, a lorry comes and collects them. Empty bottle banks are put back in their place.

7. The lorry takes the full bottle banks to a bottle warehouse.

8. The glass is stored until the glass factory is ready to take it.

PICKLES

THE LIFE-CYCLE OF A BOTTLE

15. You buy bottles and jars of your favourite food and drinks. Soon they are empty and ready to go round again!

14. The finished bottles are sold to people who make food and drinks.

13. The new bottles are checked to see if they've been made properly. Badly made bottles go back to be melted down again.

12. The gobs are moulded into the right shapes.

11. The melted glass is cut into chunks called gobs which are the right size to be made into bottles.

9. At the glass factory, the glass is crushed up. Magnets and cleaning machines take out all the bits of metal and plastic.

10. The crushed glass or cullet as it's called is heated up until it melts.

Most bottles and jars are used just once and are then thrown away! Some bottles are recycled. You pay a deposit on some bottles of fruit drinks.

Very often, careless people throw these away. If you collected them and returned them, you would make money and help to save glass!

WHAT TO DO...

1. Always buy returnable bottles if you can.

2. Check up on your local shops to find out which types of bottles they will take back.

3. Write down what you find out in your recycling notebook.

4. Collect up all of your empty bottles and ask your neighbours if they have any.
Take any returnable bottles back to the right shops and take the others to the bottle bank.

Broken glass can be used for all sorts of surprising things. In America and in some parts of Europe, glass is used to make roads. It is crushed into tiny pieces and is used like gravel.

This is called glassphalt. It reflects headlight beams, making the road easier to see at night.

GLASS can do all sorts of jobs!

Factories can make all of these things out of old glass...

bricks for building houses...

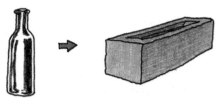

and tiles for bathrooms...

and sandpaper for smoothing wood...

SHINE!

and fibre glass for furniture and boats.

You can use jars for lots of things...

OLD NAILS

BENT NAILS

TOE NAILS

To keep your nuts and bolts in.

Try to think of more uses for your bottles and jars. Write down your ideas in your recycling notebook.

Paint them and use them as vases for flowers.

Every bottle you rescue from this dustbin is valuable to us all!

WHY?..

BOTTLE RESCUE...

SAVES ENERGY

It takes less fuel to make new glass from old bottles than from raw materials.

1 tonne of old glass used → saves 136 litres of oil

SAVES MONEY

Each bottle put in a bottle bank is one less for a dustman to collect. It costs money to collect rubbish.

SAVES RESOURCES

Using old glass to make new glass means we use less of our raw materials.

PROTECTS THE ENVIRONMENT

Less digging or quarrying for raw materials.

WHAT TO DO...

1. Always try to buy your drinks in returnable bottles.

2. Take your other bottles and jars to a bottle bank.

TRY THIS TONGUE-TWISTER

RETURNABLE BOTTLES BEAT BOTTLE BANKS, BUT BOTH ARE BETTER THAN BROKEN BOTTLES IN BINS!

THE PAPER MOUNTAIN

The abominable paperman!

A lot of the stuff we throw away is made of paper and cardboard. Most of this cardboard is packaging, like your cornflakes box and your milk carton. In Britain, about 7,000,000 tonnes of paper and cardboard are used every year. 2,000,000 tonnes are recycled. That leaves 5,000,000 tonnes which are just thrown away! Wood from trees is used to make a lot of this. We would have to cut down about 65,000,000 trees to make the paper and cardboard that we throw away every year. We need trees for more reasons than just making paper. Turn the page and take a look...

HORROR STORIES?

You do? Well, read on...

The following facts are more deadly than Dracula, more frightening than Frankenstein, more worrying than The Wolfman! Because they are all true, and happening RIGHT NOW!

FACT ONE

One square kilometre of the earth's forests is being destroyed every two minutes!...

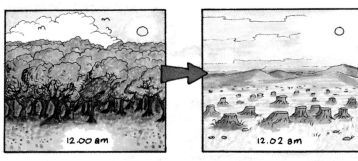

Most forests are cut down to make room for food crops, but we also cut down a lot of trees to make paper.

FACT TWO

Many animals can only live in forests. When we cut down trees, we take away their homes, so many of them DIE!..

FACT THREE

Trees give off oxygen, so forests are important for keeping up the supply of air that we breathe!..

SNIFF!

Even the plants in your house produce life-giving oxygen.

FACT FOUR

For every 1000 trees we cut down, we only plant 25 in their place. If we carry on this way, soon there won't be any trees left at all!

WHAT YOU CAN DO...

1. Look in your phone book for waste paper merchants. Write down their names and addresses in your notebook.

2. Save all your waste paper and cardboard.

3. Try to get your teacher or club leader to start a collection of paper and cardboard.

4. Make sure you keep your paper dry and store it well away from fires.

5. When you have run out of space to store the paper, ask an adult to take it to the paper merchant.

The paper merchant will sell it to a factory which will use it to make some more paper.

SAVE PAPER and you'll help to SAVE TREES and SAVE WILDLIFE!

MAKING THE MOST OF METALS

Sooner or later, we will use up all of the Earth's metals unless we try to save them.

Some experts say that metals could run out in about 100 years if we use them up as quickly as we do now.

Luckily, metals are very easy to recycle! Here are some of the more common metals you may find...

ALUMINIUM

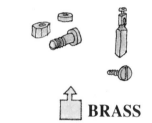

BRASS

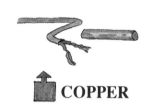

COPPER

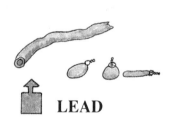

LEAD

IRON

STEEL

WHAT TO DO

Learn to identify these metals. Make notes of their uses in your notebook.

You can sell all your old scrap metal to scrap metal merchants.

Find out if there's one near your home.

Write the names and addresses of metal dealers in your notebook.

When you've collected a few kilos of metal, get an adult to take you along to a scrap metal dealer to sell it.

SAVE METAL, STOP LITTER, MAKE MONEY

METAL MERCHANTS

Scrap metal dealers sell the metal they collect to metal working factories. They often crush it into large blocks first to make it easier to transport. Sometimes, you can tell what a block was made from by examining it closely.
Why don't you try it?..

BLOX QUIZ

Here are some blocks made of compacted scrap metal. What were they? Match each of the names on the right to a block on the left.

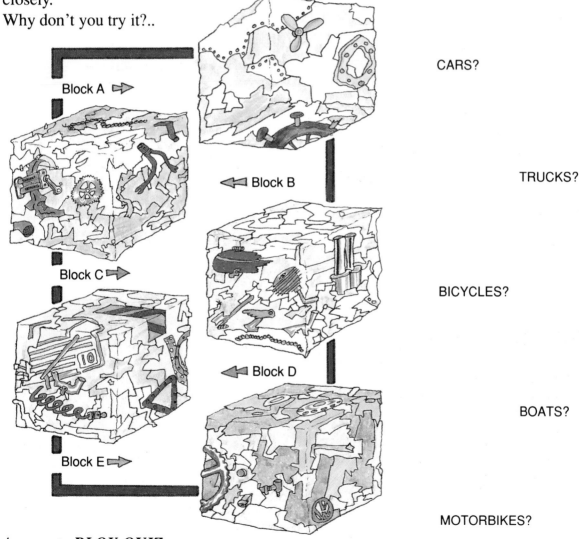

Block A

Block B

Block C

Block D

Block E

CARS?

TRUCKS?

BICYCLES?

BOATS?

MOTORBIKES?

*Answer to **BLOX QUIZ:***

A=BOATS, B=BICYCLES, C=MOTORBIKES, D=TRUCKS, E=CARS

MORE METAL FACTS

Did you know that there is almost no tin in a tin can? Tin is far too expensive to be used for making cans which are thrown away!

In America, 110 billion food and drink cans are bought each year!

It takes up to 31 barrels of oil to make 1 tonne of aluminium. When scrap aluminium is recycled, it only takes 2 barrels of oil. Some drink cans are made from valuable aluminium. Some are made from steel.

What did you do with the last empty can you had?..

LOOK! A Save-a-Can Bank!..

These work like bottle banks. Why not try to set one up at your school?

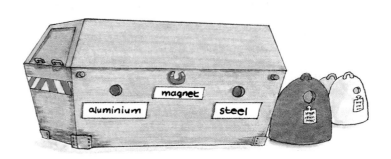

WHAT TO DO

1. Use the magnet to check which metal the cans are made of. The magnet will stick to steel cans, but not to aluminium ones.

2. Empty cans take up a lot of space. You'll need to flatten your old cans with a mallet before you put them in the bins. Watch out for your fingers!

3. When the dustbins are full ask an adult to take them to the scrap metal dealer.

FROM RAGS TO RICHES!

Try not to think of old clothes as being just useless rags. Remember...rubbish is only rubbish if you THINK it is!

● **RAG FACT**

Did you know that old rags are used in the making of bank notes? That really is rags to riches!

● Charity shops will be pleased to have your clean old clothes.

● You can take your old clothes to jumble sales. Look in the local newspaper to find out where and on what dates they take place. Write down your jumble sale information in your notebook.

● **RAG FACT**

Some cloth makers buy old clothes and shred them to make material for new clothes.
Part of the jumper you're wearing right now might be made of the old socks you threw out last year!..

Wow!

● When you grow out of old clothes, you could pass them on to friends or younger members of your family.

Plastic is cheap and easy to use. Just about anything can be made from plastic these days.

Plastic is a great invention.

BUT...it gives us a lot of **PROBLEMS!**

Most plastic is made from oil. We are using up our supplies of oil at a frightening speed.

When plastic is made, poisonous wastes and gases can escape into the environment.

It's not easy to recycle plastic. So it gets buried or burnt. That means more pollution.

The easiest plastic to identify is called PET. No, it's not a dog or a cat or a fish! It's short for...

POLYETHYLENETEREPHTHALATE

This is almost as hard to say as ...

FLOCCIPAUCINIHILIPILIFICATION
Which is the longest word in the Oxford English Dictionary.

PET is used to make strong, clear plastic bottles. Most bottles of fruit drinks are made of this sort of plastic. Until a few years ago, all fruit drink bottles were made of glass. BUT... lazy people didn't take their bottles back, so supermarkets started to sell throwaway bottles because they were cheaper. So now its getting hard to buy returnable glass bottles anywhere!

You can help to solve the plastic problem...

● These are used just like returnable glass bottles in some countries.

Always try to buy returnable glass bottles. Try to think of ways to use plastic bottles instead of throwing them away.

HOW TO GROW A PET PLANT

● You can use empty PET bottles to grow plants in.

1. Cut a bottle in half and make a few holes in each half.

2. Put soil and compost from your heap (page 12) in the bottom half.

3. Put it on an old saucer. Make holes in the soil and put your seeds in.

4. After a few weeks the plant begins to grow.

5. Stick the top half back on to protect the plant.

6. Enjoy your PET plant!

Keep the soil damp by watering it through the screw top.

WHAT'S LEFT

Most rubbish can be recycled, but you can't recycle all of it by yourself.

OIL

A lot of waste oil is poured into drains, causing pollution. Some garages collect old oil which can be cleaned and used again.

SAWDUST

Sawdust collected from woodyards can be recycled to make chipboard for furniture. Sawdust is also sold in pet shops. You can use it for cat-litter and to keep your rabbit warm in Winter!

WASTE FOOD

You can use some waste food on your compost heap. Pig farmers often buy leftover food from school dinners to feed their pigs!

By now you should be an expert recycler!
Here's a quiz to test your knowledge...

EXPERT'S EXAM

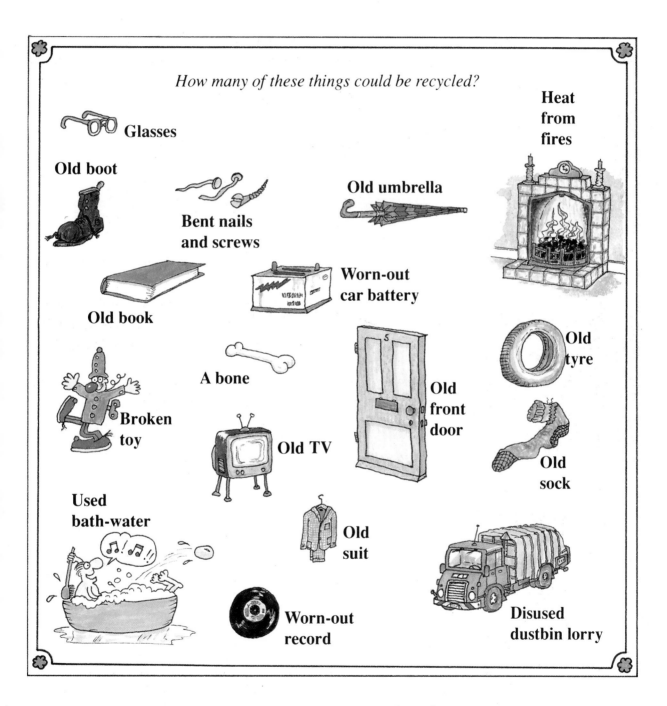

How many of these things could be recycled?

Glasses

Old boot

Bent nails and screws

Old umbrella

Heat from fires

Old book

Worn-out car battery

A bone

Old front door

Old tyre

Broken toy

Old TV

Old sock

Used bath-water

Old suit

Worn-out record

Disused dustbin lorry

*Answer to **EXPERT'S EXAM**: Everything!*

It's up to all of us to take care of the Earth. It's our home...

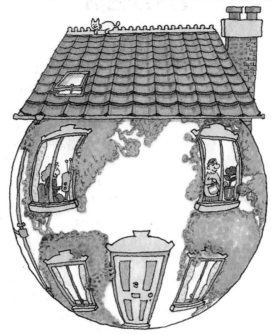

Recycling can help save our supplies and keep our world safer and healthier!
Recycling means keeping your dustbin as empty as possible!

Remember...
1. Recycle as much as you can.
2. Tell your friends about recycling.
3. Get other people to collect paper, bottles and cans.
4. Think before you throw ANYTHING away!

Every little helps.
NOW...

HOW ARE YOU GOING TO RECYCLE THIS BOOK?